Understanding

Child Sexual Abuse

Therapeutic Guidelines for Professionals
Working with Children

by

Thom L. McGuire

and

Faye E. Grant

Butterworths
Toronto   Vancouver

Understanding Child Sexual Abuse
© 1991 Butterworths Canada Ltd.

Printed and bound in Canada

The Butterworth Group of Companies

Canada
Butterworths Canada Ltd., 75 Clegg Road, MARKHAM, Ont. L6G 1A1 and 409 Granville Street, Suite 1455, VANCOUVER, B.C. V6C 1T2
Australia
Butterworths Pty Ltd., SYDNEY, MELBOURNE, BRISBANE, ADELAIDE, PERTH, CANBERRA and HOBART
Ireland
Butterworth (Ireland) Ltd., DUBLIN
New Zealand
Butterworth of New Zealand Ltd., WELLINGTON and AUCKLAND
Puerto Rico
Equity de Puerto Rico, Inc., HATO REY
Singapore
Malayan Law Journal Pte. Ltd., SINGAPORE
United Kingdom
Butterworth & Co. (Publishers) Ltd., LONDON and EDINBURGH
United States
Butterworth Legal Publishers, AUSTIN, Texas; BOSTON, Massachusetts; CLEARWATER, Florida (D & S Publishers); ORFORD, New Hampshire (Equity Publishing); ST. PAUL, Minnesota; and SEATTLE, Washington.

Canadian Cataloguing in Publication Data

McGuire, Thom
  Understanding child sexual abuse

Includes index.
ISBN 0-409-89771-X

1. Sexually abused children. 2. Sexually abused children – Services for. I. Grant, Faye E. (Faye Edith), 1940–   . II. Title.

HQ71.M34 1990   362.7'6   C90-095656-9

Sponsoring editor: Fran Cudlipp
Editor: Anne Lynas Shah
Cover design: Brant Cowie
Production: Kevin Skinner

Preface

Child sexual abuse is not simply a clinical problem or a legal problem. It is a social problem afflicting thousands of Canadian children every year. It is estimated that one in four girls and one in six boys will experience uninvited sexual contact by the age of eighteen years.

The dilemma facing child protection workers is twofold. First, there are an overwhelming number of disclosures and the need to respond accordingly. Second, validating these disclosures requires competency beyond the level of simply understanding the issues. Never before in the history of social services has there been an issue which has created the level of discomfort experienced by social workers, police, and Crown counsel.

Child sexual abuse intervention requires a level of coordination which is both demanding and at times exhausting. Professionals at all levels of a child's life play a crucial role in determining a successful outcome. This includes mental health workers (treatment needs), health care professionals (physical health), police (investigation), social service personnel (child protection), and those involved in education (social learning).

This book is designed to assist those professionals involved with children who are victims of sexual abuse. While the issues are complex and varied, we are attempting to define major areas of consideration for the individual worker, in whatever capacity, when intervening with children and their families. Such considerations include developing a personal level of comfort, agency coordination, assessing treatment needs, and counselling. Special circumstances are discussed with emphasis on when the offender is in a position of trust, and recommendations are given regarding false allegations.

The information provided in this book is limited with the intended purpose of providing basic facts. The material is confined to outlining a summary of the more important therapeutic concerns related to practical issues confronting professionals.

In conclusion, it is our hope that this book will provide useful material for all professionals who work with children. It is our belief that through creative intervention, assistance in these difficult cases can ease the burden on individual professionals, whether social workers, child and youth care counsellors, educators, or investigators, and, more importantly, on child victims of sexual abuse.

Acknowledgements

The authors gratefully acknowledge the assistance of Dr. Kloh-Ann Amacher, Professor of Social Work at the University of British Columbia, Ms. Vicki Henderson, Coordinator of The Children's Foundation, and Dr. E. Michael Coles, Professor of Psychology at Simon Fraser University for their review and suggestions.

We sincerely appreciate our families for their support and patience throughout this project.

This book is dedicated to all victims of sexual abuse. May their courage be an inspiration to all.

Table of Contents

CHAPTER ONE

Sexual Abuse of Children, An Overview

As a social problem, child sexual abuse reports have increased dramatically in the last five years. Experts agree that we are only seeing conservative estimates as incidence studies suggest that one in four females and one in six males experience unwanted sexual acts. A federal commission on the study of sexual offences against children reports that one in two females and one in three males experience sexual victimization. According to this commission, 80 percent of these victims are children. It seems evident that the number of reports seen by investigators are far fewer than the claims of these studies. This is not to suggest that investigations are incomplete, but rather that a number of children do not disclose. However, as professionals begin to educate children through the classroom setting and the media, this is changing.

Although great effort has been put forth in educating children in personal safety, there is still a great deal of information unknown. We do, however, know that most incidents of sexual abuse occur between the child and a known, trusted adult. Sexual abuse by a stranger appears to account for only about 15 percent of the cases. The current epidemic surrounding child sexual abuse may be due to an increase in reports. Since the revelation of the "battered child syndrome" in 1962, child protection as a social policy is included in all provincial child welfare legislation. Reporting laws are mandatory across Canada, and it has only been in the last ten years that child sexual abuse has become recognized and statistically recorded.

This is not to suggest that the process has not been without problems. Child abuse is a difficult topic to acknowledge. Rarely are members of our society comfortable in confronting sexuality. When the topics of sexuality and abuse combine, they make for a very powerful situation. We live in a very sexually stereotyped society which has a dramatic influence on our behaviour. We have a whole set of attitudes about the sanctity of the family, particularly women and children. The issues relating to moral standards surrounding sexuality are highly controversial. One is either for or against sexual expression, and consequently, such polarization contributes to the secret keeping involved in child sexual abuse.

Professionals often talk about sexual abuse as an abuse of power. The offender is seen as exercising his or her power over the child. It is important to understand the dynamics of power and how it relates to this topic. In terms of the relationship between an adult and a child, power is inherent. Adults have power through physical size, authority, and their intellectual abilities as well as through material possessions. They exercise this power in many socially acceptable avenues. Children are taught to respect adult authority in a variety of settings. It is because "good" children are expected to comply with adult authority that professionals can begin to understand how easy it is for offenders to take advantage of their position.

As professionals undertake the enormous responsibility of intervening on behalf of children, they can be expected to confront the status quo. We live in a patriarchal society where children are afforded very few rights. Unfortunately, many of our prevention efforts are aimed at the child. This is difficult because one has to be careful when suggesting to a child that personal power exists when in fact it does not. In examining our prevention efforts, individuals involved in child advocacy must also focus their efforts on what it is about our society that creates such a curious paradox. There is an unstated value that adult-child sex is taboo, but this does not concur with how often it occurs.

There is a tendency to treat child sexual abuse similarly to physical abuse, as a mental health problem. Few cases of physical abuse come to the attention of the criminal courts. Often apprehensions of children are seen in Family Court, where coordination efforts are easily accessible. Child sexual abuse is different in that intervention efforts require the cooperation of a number of investigative bodies. The *Criminal Code* clearly defines illegal sexual behaviours (see Appendix I) and, therefore, child protection workers need to coordinate their efforts with law enforcement, Crown counsel, and in some cases, medical health officers attached to community care licensing boards. Perhaps physical abuse and neglect should be treated in the same manner.

The effects of child sexual abuse are individual and depend on a variety of factors:

a) the nature of the sexual abuse
b) the frequency and duration of the abuse
c) the relationship between the victim and the offender
d) the developmental level of the child
e) the gender of the child and offender
f) the age difference between child and offender
g) the level of secrecy and dependency
h) the dynamics surrounding disclosure
i) the rewards/reinforcers offered to the child
j) physical sensations versus internal discomfort in the child

k) degree of family/outside support (belief, safety, and control)
l)   degree of responsibility experienced by the child
m) the child's previous background.

Each of these factors can affect individual children differently. Some may be more relevant than others. It is helpful for child professionals to be cognizant of them.

DISCLOSURE

Both legally and therapeutically, disclosure of child sexual abuse is the most critical component of any investigation. From a legal point of view, courts consider disclosure to be key evidence. From a therapeutic point of view, how the listener reacts can severely affect the level of trauma experienced by the child. When faced with the decision, most children do not disclose. Most children are aware that sexual activity between an adult and child is inappropriate. When confronted with an abusive/ exploitive adult, children can assume responsibility for the activity. As a result, the disclosure becomes a key clinical factor. Children will disclose sexual abuse in several ways:

a) *Direct communication*: The child is direct in communicating the abuse to a trusted adult.
b) *The victim tells someone else*: The child tells a friend or school chum, often eliciting secrecy.
c) *The clue*: The child hints at a non-specific problem, usually not directly.
d) *Signs and symptoms*: Behavioural and emotional indicators (discussed in Chapter Two).

Children fear disclosure due to repercussions of disbelief and/or blame. In many cases this has been reinforced by the offender. Consequently, children arrive at the conclusion not to disclose. Many feel frightened and powerless which, over time, creates a sense of helplessness.

It is very difficult for children to accuse the offender, particularly if the offender is a family member or trusted friend. Children find it painful to betray a relationship which had been based on trust and loyalty. The only power children possess in this exploitive relationship is in maintaining the secret. If exposing the secret implies the threat of abandonment, then most children remain silent. When children do not feel they have the option to disclose, they will often seek a means of coping with the exploitive relationship. Unfortunately, most coping techniques available to children are criticized by other adults in the community and often lead to stigmatization.

In order to cope, some children resort to drugs and/or alcohol and are unable to comply with the demands of school. As a result, they are labelled delinquent. By the time the child does disclose, he or she is met with disbelief because of past inappropriate activity. The same is true when a child exhibits behavioural and emotional problems. It is difficult for adults to be tolerant and believe a child who has a history of acting out or regressive/withdrawn behaviours. Child professionals must be aware of these considerations when faced with a disclosure. It takes a great deal of courage to disclose and the level of trauma induced in the child should not be underestimated. Retraction can also result when a child's disclosure is met with adverse reaction as most children are unprepared for the chaos surrounding an initial investigation.

Professionals should respond to disclosure in a calm, rational manner. While abused children are used to accommodating adults in their life, they will often be acutely aware of offering only as much information as they think the adult can handle. It is important that adults not agree to promise secrecy when requested by the child. Children will often begin a disclosure by asking, "If I tell you this, will you promise not to tell?" One must be careful of the response and inform children that one is unable to make such promises if their health and safety are concerned. Such statements can be made very empathically in order to ensure the child's trust. Professionals do not want to have to maintain confidentiality when they are legally mandated to report. Similarly, adults receiving a disclosure will need to consider creative methods of reporting while maintaining the child's cooperation. Along with stating legal obligations to the child, adults can express their need for additional help in this matter, and then contact the investigative agencies.

EFFECTS

In understanding the nature of the sexual abuse, child professionals have to be careful not to be judgmental. Individual children respond differently depending on the relationship between the offender and the child. The closer the relationship, the greater the degree of trauma. To a girl, being fondled by her father could be equally as traumatic as rape by a stranger. The frequency and duration of the abuse can offer some indications of the level of secrecy held by the child. Adolescents in particular have a more difficult time divulging the abuse because there is a likelihood of lengthy involvement. Knowledge regarding the developmental level of the child assists child professionals in choosing an appropriate method of intervention.

Sometimes the effects of sexual abuse are related to gender. Since most sexual offenders are male, boys may experience fears associated with sexual identity. This is also true if the offender is female. If a boy experiences sexual abuse by an adult female, he can be caught in a double bind. There is pressure that the sexual relationship should have been enjoyable and, if the male child experiences this relationship as traumatic, it could further reinforce homosexual ideation. This is reflected in public attitude. If a young boy is sexually abused by an adult male, there is fear that he might become homosexual. If a young girl is sexually abused by an adult male, the fear is that she might hate men and/or sex. The implications, that the little boy liked the experience and turns toward it while the little girl hated the experience and turns away from it, are myths requiring further education. Such belief systems are based on male/female socialization and need to be challenged. Similarly, male victims tend to externalize such effects. Boys are taught, from a very young age, to withhold feelings, be in control, and take care of themselves. Consequently, disclosure has been viewed as weak and unmasculine.

The age difference between the child and the offender is critical both legally and emotionally. Up until recently, the sexual acts of adolescent offenders had been thought of in terms of normal child sexual exploration. This has changed dramatically as knowledge increases, and consequently, laws have changed in this area (see Appendix I). What becomes important is the difference in the ages between the child and offender. It is possible that young offenders are more likely to be involved in physical force as they are less adept at exhibiting coercive abilities. They are also less likely to resort to disinhibitors such as alcohol and/or drugs prior to offending.

Whatever the offender's age, the effects of sexual abuse experienced by the child appear to be more traumatic with increased levels of secrecy and dependency. Whatever rewards and reinforcers used in eliciting the child's cooperation add to the child's feelings of responsibility, guilt and shame. Many children feel responsible for the abuse simply because their body responded to the physical sensations. Trauma results in the child's inability to separate internal feelings of discomfort from the external physical sensations.

Much of the adverse effects of sexual abuse are highly individualized and can sometimes depend on the child's previous background and emotional health, degree of outside support, and the ability of the family to establish belief, safety, and control following disclosure.

OFFENDERS

Sexual offenders are not all the same. There are many myths surrounding the profile of the offender as it is difficult to do comprehensive research. Most studies use sample populations from treatment facilities or penal institutions; thus, information is isolated. There are limited data available on sexual offenders who have not come into contact with authorities. However, despite these limitations, many experts in forensic psychology, psychiatry, and social work have developed a number of theories related to sexual offenders. Professionals will benefit from exploring the recent literature.

Allowing for theoretical differences, a sexual offender pattern may include denial (of the offence), rationalization, minimization, and projection. Behavioural psychologists have described the personality of the child sexual offender as egocentric, immature, impulsive, and sometimes developmentally arrested. Few sexual offenders are mentally ill. Most function adequately in their jobs, social activities, and within a family, although many are seen as quite authoritative.

Distinctions have been made between the motivation of the sexual offender and the type of offences committed. Although rape and exhibitionism are seen on a continuum representing extremes, there appear to be major differences regarding the drive. The primary purpose of adults who engage in sexual contact with children is not necessarily sexual. Fear of age mates and developmental immaturity sometimes lead offenders into seeking approval, affection, companionship and intimacy from less threatening individuals.

A possible explanation for why the majority of sexual offenders are male involves socialization. Young male adolescents are taught that future relationships are not equal. Men should be taller, stronger, and more dominant than their partners. Unfortunately, there are some who believe that these attributes are not only important, but vital. They seek relationships which would allow them the maximum amount of control. Yet sexual involvement and, to a greater degree, intimacy involve giving up some of that power and control. Threatened by the loss of authority and the desire to seek intimacy, some males seek out sexual relationships where they can maintain this control. Children fulfil that need as most children do not have the knowledge to consent or the power to resist.

A typology of sexual offenders is useful in making distinctions between offences committed and offender impulsion. Dr. A. Nicholas Groth, author of *Men Who Rape* and director of the sexual offender program at the Connecticut Correctional Institution in Somers, developed a typology of child molesters and rapists. Rapists are distinguished in three categories: anger, power, and sadism. Child molesters are distinguished in two categories: fixated and regressed. The fixated paedophile's primary sexual orientation is toward children. His victims are mainly male and the sexual offences usually occur outside the family. The fixated molester closely identifies with his victims, bringing himself to the level of the child, not unlike a peer relationship. Most offences are premeditated and there is often no history of alcohol or drug abuse. The offence is viewed as a result of developmental immaturity.

According to Groth, the regressed molester's primary sexual orientation is toward age mates. His victims are usually female and offences often occur within the family. The regressed molester, through a process of substitution, places the child victims in adult roles. Offences may be more episodic and initially impulsive. The offence is viewed by Groth as a result of maladaptive responses to life stresses.

Behavioural research suggests that sexual offenders begin a process of deviant sexual fantasy in adolescence. These fantasies are self-reinforced through masturbatory behaviour and become deviant arousal patterns. For these reasons, intervention with adolescent offenders can be viewed as primary prevention.

Many sexual offenders seek an ongoing relationship with a child. Dependencies are created and the offences are considered by the offender to be secure and reciprocal. The offender rationalizes his behaviour as needing to educate the child for future sexual experiences. Further, he feels he is the only person who truly cares. As a result of his egocentricity, lack of empathy, and impulsivity, he is unlikely to consider the consequences. The offender may also feel that the child is simply an extension of himself and exercise ownership as his right. This is common to incestuous families where children are often isolated from peers and the community; the mother is often as much a victim as the children.

The offender will also minimize and deny his behaviour as a coping mechanism to manage personal distress. This could be a result of outside influences or internal guilt. Offenders will minimize their behaviours by denying the extent and/or frequency of the abuse. This is not unlike children when they first disclose. When first confronted, denial is not surprising because most adults do not want to believe that someone they know and trust would be involved in such behaviour. It is easier to believe the offender's denial than to accept that what the child is saying is true. There are more false denials than false allegations.

Finally, projection is often used in diverting blame away from the offender and toward others. This is seen when the child is characterized as being "seductive" or "sexually aggressive". Further responsibility is sometimes directed toward the offender's spouse, family, employer or any other source of stress.

Children are enticed into an exploitive relationship by threats, bribes, rewards, coercion, and manipulation. A common response in eliciting compliance involves making the child responsible for harm to the offender and the family:

"If anybody finds out about this I'll really be in trouble. They could send me to jail."

> "If your mother finds out, she'll be really upset. You'll be sent to a foster home and the rest of the family will be on welfare."

A further example involves the offender's reliance on the "special' relationship:

> "Nobody understands how much we care about each other."

> "It is important for people who like each other to feel good."

Bribery and rewards not only involve material possessions but can also include special attention and recognition.

Understanding certain dynamics as well as offender motivation is useful when handling a disclosure. This will give some insight into the difficulties faced by children as they consider the consequences of telling. Anticipating what was said by the offender can assist in choosing the types of questions required for an assessment. Behavioural indicators will often provide clues to the professional when the offender is discussed.

CHAPTER TWO

Awareness and Intervention

A PERSONAL EVALUATION

Prior to becoming involved, child professionals need to evaluate their own philosophical framework. Theoretical assumptions vary according to an individual's training and experience. Unlike most crimes, child sexual abuse stirs up a great deal of emotion at all levels of professional involvement. An important factor in generating a successful outcome is recognizing and identifying issues that inhibit a comfortable approach. Even in everyday matters, it is difficult to separate personal and professional concerns. When intervening in child sexual abuse cases the boundaries separating emotion from intellect become extremely blurred. While one is not expected to have these issues clarified prior to any involvement, it is helpful to acknowledge and be aware of their presence. Increased awareness allows professionals to intercept and effect positive change.

An initial step in becoming comfortable involves evaluating personal feelings related to child sexual abuse. It is through self-awareness that the child professional can maintain objectivity. This is important because of the legal implications surrounding leading questions. The emotional impact, the level of involvement, and the response of the professional all severely affect the level of trauma experienced by the child. As a result, it becomes crucial that the individual develop a personal level of comfort because one can never predict what information will be revealed.

INTROSPECTION

Child professionals must be prepared for a wide range of feelings when confronted with these cases. Emotions such as shock, denial, disbelief, anger, pity, and disgust are all normal reactions from most adults, especially when the situation opposes the myths surrounding personal belief systems. When growing up most people remember being warned of the "stranger" or the "schoolyard pervert", but thought this was a rare phenomenon. Present-day knowledge surrounding the extent of sexual abuse and incest conflicts with past perceptions. It is for these reasons that professionals involved with victims keep up to date with current findings.

Very few crimes evoke the types of reactions associated with child molestation. Even in prison, murderers maintain a higher status amongst inmates than sexual offenders. One explanation came from an inmate who was a bank robber: he said that what his crime was is what he did; what the sexual offender did is what he is. An individual's feelings associated with disclosure are similar to those experienced by a parent. Denial and disbelief are not surprising as the child assumes fault and the offender denies involvement.

It is this institutionalized thinking which reinforces such reactions and makes it difficult for the professional to maintain objectivity. Shock is a reaction which can severely hinder the outcome of the intervention. How the adult reacts can affect the trust level exhibited by the child. Note taking, focusing on the child's brow, eliciting an empathic response, and allowing breaks are some techniques to permit the child professional to recuperate. Another common problem lies in the adult over-identifying with the child. Caution needs to be exercised so the child does not interpret this response as pity or sympathy.

Finally, individuals dealing with the child must learn methods to recognize and identify their own anger and disgust. This is particularly important when confronted with incest as one must never assume that the relationship between the child and the offender is a negative one. While sexual offences against children offend our sense of fairness, it is critical that our anger and disgust are dealt with prior to the interaction and not during.

OBJECTIVITY

Objectivity is one of the hardest positions to maintain. Most professionals involved in child protection are also child advocates. It is difficult not to want to rescue, particularly when intervening with victims of sexual abuse who can appear so vulnerable. Ironically, an objective approach is what is necessary to meet the needs of the child and create an environment that is safe and predictable.

In order to maintain objectivity the individual must have knowledge of sexual abuse dynamics. It is important to understand common events following disclosure, offender patterns, the extent of abuse, and needs of the victim. Insight into these matters will assist in developing a framework from which to assess. While one increases knowledge on general facts surrounding child sexual abuse, one is also less likely to be caught off guard. Although feelings will always arise, objectivity increases with experience. If one becomes nervous or agitated, a common response is to increase the level of conversation. Consequently, questions become unfocused and there is a danger of leading the child into responding in a manner inappropriate to the task at hand.

All disclosures must be investigated by professionals who have the authority and mandate. Child professionals should not conduct the investigation themselves but rather, when met with a first disclosure, report to child protection agencies and the police. If it becomes necessary to ask questions, one should consider the possibility of a criminal investigation and exercise caution when responding. In order to protect the integrity of a possible investigation, one should refrain from asking leading questions which may later be interpreted as being suggestive.

LEADING QUESTIONS

Leading questions are those which elicit a response from the child which is based more on the information interpreted by the professional than on the child's own experience. It only has to be perceived as such for the questions to be seen as leading. If dealing with an initial disclosure, individuals need to contemplate the types of questions appropriate to the child's developmental level. Abstaining from leading the child serves two purposes: the investigation becomes legally sound and there is a greater likelihood of a truthful disclosure.

The following are examples of similar questions considered leading and non-leading:

LEADING QUESTIONS	NON-LEADING QUESTIONS
"Did he touch you on the penis or the bum?"	"Where did he touch you?"
"Did Uncle Joe hurt you?"	"Who hurt you?"
"Did he put his penis in your mouth?"	"Can you tell me what happened?"
"Did it happen before or after you went to bed?"	"Around what time did it happen?"
"Did you feel scared?"	"How did you feel?"
"I'm here to help you because I understand bad things happened to you. Your mother told me that you want to talk about sexual abuse."	"I'm here to help you and I wonder if we could talk. What would you like to talk about?"
"Do you know what a vagina is?"	"Tell me what you call the private parts of your body."
"Did she take off your clothes?"	"Were you dressed?"

Leading questions can inadvertently give children a vocabulary previously unknown to them. This could result in loss of credibility both in the child's evidence and the skills of the child professional.

PERSONAL LEVEL OF COMFORT

Professionals need to develop a personal level of comfort in order to adequately intervene in the lives of victims of sexual abuse. There are a number of ways in which this can be achieved but, overall, the issues are personal to the individual involved. The following are a series of questions designed to assist in resolving matters which may inhibit personal comfort. Questions for consideration include the following:

1. How is sexuality dealt with in my family? How was sexuality expressed by my mother? How was sexuality expressed by my father?
2. Did I talk about sex openly with my family or with my friends?
3. How did I view sex as a child? How does this affect me at present?
4. Was I or were any of my friends sexually abused? Does this hinder my professional objectivity?
5. What are the normal ways families express sexuality in the home?
6. Are children sexual?
7. What is wrong with adult-child sex?
8. What is normal child sex play?
9. Do I react differently to the topic of child sexual abuse professionally than I do personally?
10. What are my attitudes about women? men? children? sex roles? rape? wife battering? homosexuality?
11. What are the ethical considerations?

As one explores the above questions, an opportunity exists to critically examine present-day values related to the professionals' role. It is important to have an openness about human diversity in order to intervene effectively. Self-awareness is a major component in developing a personal level of comfort.

DEVELOPMENTAL LEVEL OF THE CHILD

Professionals involved in sexual abuse should be aware of the developmental considerations related to the child. It is important to have a concept of what is "normal" and what type of behaviour is appropriate to the child's age level. Children are not little adults, and it is crucial that assumptions are not based on lack of knowledge. While not all children develop at the same rate, there are predictable stages useful for this discussion. Understanding the developmental issues assists child professionals in their choice of questions and is also beneficial to an initial assessment.

In order to clarify the developmental stages, it is useful to consider the child's cognitive, behavioural, and emotional progress.

Pre-School

Children of pre-school age are extremely egocentric and view themselves in terms of their immediate surroundings. They are emotionally spontaneous yet have the ability to distinguish truth from fiction. It is difficult for pre-schoolers to understand cause and effect relationships. Their memories do not necessarily follow a chronological order and they have particular problems with time and space. It is especially important that professionals refrain from abstract notions because children of this age may leave the impression that the message is understood when in fact it is not. Usually one can expect pre-schoolers to be very outgoing and energetic; however, the trauma of abuse can result in withdrawn and fearful behaviour. Caution should be exercised in that highly developed verbal skills may not necessarily imply equal levels of comprehension. Most pre-schoolers view adults in their world as having complete control over the events in their lives. While these children will lie to get out of trouble and sex is often comprehended in terms of "poo-poo" and "pee-pee", it is unlikely that their level of sophistication would involve explicit sexual fantasy.

School Age

As young children develop a greater sense of others around them, their priorities begin to shift from family commitment to relating to peers. School-aged children are easily embarrassed and have difficulty expressing their emotions in words. As a result of developing a sense of modesty, it is not uncommon for children of this age to behave in a rather silly way when discussing sexuality. Their level of comprehension becomes fairly sophisticated and, therefore, they have a good sense of time and space.

Adolescence

Typically, adolescence is a time of confusion and frustration. As adolescents develop through pubescence, a sexual awakening often leads to mixed emotions. The adolescent is physically maturing. Combined with the struggle between family commitment and personal autonomy, this developmental phase is unlike any other. It is important to understand that, in conjunction with significant physical changes, the adolescent is also undergoing a great deal of emotional upheaval and may question family values. Professionals can expect close ties to a peer group and it is possible that there is limited compatibility with adults. Adolescents are developmentally capable of abstract concepts and the associated language.

Many are under a great deal of pressure to become sexually active and they are almost always aware of issues surrounding sexuality; however, their information may not always be correct. It must be understood that the cognitive, emotional, and behavioural abilities of adolescents vary greatly. This is especially true in the case of sexual abuse victims. One can expect a continuum of responses ranging from sullen, withdrawn behaviour to severe acting out. A significant difference between adolescent victims of sexual abuse and younger children is that the abuse may have gone on for a far greater length of time.

BEHAVIOURAL AND EMOTIONAL INDICATORS

Child professionals must exercise caution when considering the emotional and behavioural signs indicating that sexual abuse has possibly occurred. For obvious reasons, a child's disclosure often becomes the most significant indicator. Inexperienced practitioners may mistakenly assume abuse has taken place by observing or acknowledging a wide range of signs and symptoms which may in fact have nothing to do with the suspected abuse. Children may exhibit a variety of problematic behaviours which could very well relate to family dysfunction, peer relationship problems, school difficulties, or undiagnosed physical ailments. These can take the form of interpersonal difficulties (withdrawal, aggressiveness, or poor social skills), emotional disturbance (depression, poor self-esteem, fearfulness), and somatic disorders (upset stomach, eating disorders, and night-time disturbance).

Keeping this in mind, the following is a list of possible behavioural and emotional indicators for the professional to be aware of prior to intervention. This list is not comprehensive, and it is important to note that certain signs and symptoms will only pertain to an appropriate age group.

Bedwetting	Thumb sucking
Excessive masturbation	Initiating sex play with peers
Sexual attention to pets or animals	Physically dominating

School problems—"failure to learn"

Intellectual bewilderment

Distrust of adults

Ambivalent relationship to adults

Desire to defend and be protective of oneself

Alternating behaviours: loud, hostile to affectionate, coy

Sexual, angry fantasies

Violent outbursts

Anger in play

Withdrawal

Crying a lot in sleep

Lack of appetite

Fear of outside

Dislike of baths, going to the bathroom

Changes in sleep patterns

Sexually transmitted diseases

Physical trauma in genital area

Pain around genitals or throat

Unusual offensive odour, i.e., vaginal infection

Pregnancy

Unusual interest in sexual acts

Sexual terminology

Unusually seductive behaviour

Extreme fear of showers, bathrooms, or special rooms

Refusing to undress for gym, public swimming areas

Fear of being alone with men or women

Frequent absences from school with parental consent

Repeated attempts by child to run away

Fearful of going home after school

Signs in artwork, essays (child's concepts of anatomy are skewed)

Attempts to disclose

Feelings may include ambivalence, anger, hostility, guilt, shame, fear, and frustration

Alcohol/drug abuse

Excessive eating

Aggressive behaviour

Sexual promiscuity

Prostitution

Over-compliance

Poor self-care skills

Regressive behaviours

Pseudo-maturity

Phobias

Few of these behaviours in themselves (outside of pregnancy and sexually transmitted diseases) confirm that sexual abuse has in fact occurred. It is important to understand that such signs and symptoms have to be taken into consideration with other sources which may involve the child's disclosure, medical evidence, and the circumstances.

CIRCUMSTANCES INVOLVED

The behavioural and emotional indicators pertaining to a child who has been sexually abused can be attributed to the effects of the trauma. The circumstances in which the abuse occurred must be considered as the professional should take into account a number of factors relating to the specific situation. Understanding the developmental level of the child, the extent and frequency of abuse, and the relationship between the offender and the victim can be of assistance. Increased knowledge prior to intervention can assist in developing an appropriate treatment plan.

ALLEGED OFFENDER/OFFENCES

Knowing something about the offender and the offences which have occurred can be beneficial in treatment planning, particularly if the offender is a family member, babysitter or trusted friend. How, where, and when the alleged abuse took place can also be of assistance. It is not necessary to have this information prior to the intervention but in a similar way to having some insight into the circumstances, such knowledge not only facilitates questions which can be creative and non-leading, but also helps in understanding an individual child's level of responsibility and self-blame.

CHAPTER THREE

The Professional Community Response

NETWORKING: LEGAL, MEDICAL, AND OTHER SOURCES

As a result of the sensitive nature of sexual abuse, child professionals will find it helpful to coordinate their efforts with other agencies. This varies depending on the extent of the situation surrounding the abuse. The following outlines government ministries and agencies likely to be involved in order to ensure adequate service to victims and their families:

Child protection	Legally responsible for ensuring that children are not at risk from all forms of child abuse and neglect.
Law enforcement	Legally responsible for gathering evidence and making recommendations to Crown counsel regarding criminal charges.
Crown counsel	Legally responsible for laying criminal charges, interviewing potential witnesses, and representing the Crown in criminal trials.
Medical personnel	Responsible for ensuring the health and welfare of suspected victims of sexual abuse.
Community care licensing boards	Oversee private agencies, institutions, and day cares responsible for the care of children and set standards for the level of care.
School board personnel	Have a mandate to educate, set school board policy related to reporting and internal investigations.

| Mental health professionals | Provide treatment to victims. Also provide training to other professionals and parent groups. |

In many Canadian communities, professionals form a multi-disciplinary team in an effort to coordinate communication which can assist victims of sexual abuse. Many of the mentioned disciplines are directly involved in the process. Child professionals will benefit from sharing relevant information necessary if involved in an investigation. Although investigative procedures will differ from one community to another, it is helpful to have some understanding of an agency's mandate.

Child Protection

In Canada, most child protection workers are social workers employed through a government ministry or a private society contracted to perform such services. These workers have the authority to investigate all complaints related to child abuse and neglect and, if necessary, to apprehend children to ensure their protection. Throughout the country, individual workers act on behalf of a superintendent or director of child welfare. Given the nature of sexual abuse, there are criminal elements to child protection which explains why protection workers must work cooperatively with law enforcement.

Law Enforcement

In all cases of suspected sexual abuse, the police should be contacted. It is their responsibility to assess whether a crime has been committed. Police gather evidence related to the disclosure and are interested in whether there is enough information to warrant criminal charges. They may want to know about where the abuse occurred, the frequency, if others were involved, and, more importantly, the identity of the alleged offender. While this information is similar to that gathered by child protection investigators, it is often the police who interview the offender. As a result, cooperation is essential.

Law enforcement officers have the authority to gather evidence crucial to the investigation. This includes the ability to obtain a search warrant and to confiscate relevant evidence. This evidence could include clothing, photographs and equipment (pornography), calendars, diaries, weapons, magazines, bank and employment records, and sexual aids. Other sources of evidence could include gifts given to the child as well as receipts for purchases for items such as alcohol, drugs, and videos. In a criminal trial such information is useful in determining opportunity and availability.

In many communities law enforcement officers work together with other investigative bodies at the initial interview. This is advised so that the child does not have to be repeatedly interviewed. Upon completion of their investigation, police present their evidence to Crown counsel to determine whether charges are warranted.

Crown Counsel

Crown counsel are prosecutors who represent "the people" in court during criminal proceedings. Individual prosecutors do not represent the victim *per se* but act on behalf of the Crown (i.e., government) in order that "the people" are represented. Their aim is to establish the truth. In cases of child sexual abuse, a prosecutor will be involved in interviewing and preparing the victim and potential witnesses for trial. In preparing a child for court, the prosecutor may take the child into a courtroom to acquaint him or her with the physical surroundings and dispel any fears or anxieties he or she may have. This could include explaining the various roles of court personnel (the judge, sheriff, court recorder, jury, defence lawyer and Crown), swearing an oath, and telling the truth versus fabrication. It is essential that Crown counsel participate in coordination efforts when confronted with child sexual abuse cases.

Medical Personnel

Suspected victims of sexual abuse should be examined by a medical doctor trained in performing physical examinations of this sensitive nature. This is important both from a legal and therapeutic perspective. For some children, a physical examination can lead to re-experiencing the abuse. Although rarely found, physical evidence can provide useful information for the child's well-being and to the legal system. Therapeutically, it is important to understand that many children of all ages harbour myths surrounding sexuality and their bodies. It is valuable for children to hear from a medical professional that they are physically healthy and undamaged. In any physical examination, a child may re-experience aspects of the abuse and exhibit a variety of negative emotions, such as fear, guilt and shame.

It is not the intention of this book to outline proper medical protocol in examining suspected victims; however, child professionals should know which doctors in their community are familiar with such procedures. A standardized protocol regarding medical examinations can assist with coordination efforts. This process should include procedures, equipment, and how such evidence should be gathered. This includes evidence of injury, vaginal and anal findings, presence of sperm, and sexually transmitted diseases. Given the recent awareness surrounding AIDS, one will need to be sensitive when broaching this subject. While any protocol will need to accommodate the personnel available, it is helpful to be aware of the basics. Privacy and confidentiality are very important. In any kind of physical examination, consent must be obtained from the complainant or the legal guardian.

Community Care Licensing Boards

Licensing boards have the responsibility of overseeing child care facilities and setting standards for the level of care. This may include residential treatment centres, day care centres, private schools, and even organized summer camps. In some provinces such boards are directed by a medical health officer. Licensing boards may become involved in investigating allegations of sexual abuse either when a suspected victim resides in such a facility or when an alleged offender is employed within their jurisdiction. Although the mandate of licensing boards may vary from region to region, it is essential that they become part of the process. This is important both in terms of information sharing and the protection of children within these facilities.

School Board Personnel

Educators have a mandate to educate and, as a result, have access to a large number of children over a lengthy period of time. In recent years there have been expectations on school board personnel to become aware of child abuse concerns. While mandated to report suspected cases of abuse, many schools throughout the country have included in their curriculum child abuse prevention programs. Simultaneously, superintendents and trustees have developed new policies related to these issues. Other child professionals rely on information sharing and cooperation from teachers, counsellors, and administrators in monitoring a child's individual progress. Just as investigators rely on school board personnel, the relationship is reciprocal.

School board employees are not trained nor do they have a mandate to investigate suspected cases of child sexual abuse. At times these boundaries can become blurred, particularly when the alleged offender is an employee of the board. When these situations arise, it is vital that investigative coordination include open communication, information sharing, and leadership, which should be provided by those who are mandated to exercise the necessary authority, usually law enforcement personnel or child protection workers.

Mental Health Professionals

Mental health professionals include psychiatrists, psychologists, social workers, child and youth care counsellors, school counsellors, and private therapists. Mandated to provide treatment, they are an essential component of any coordination team. They may provide direct intervention, consultation, and testing. Some may also provide training in child sexual abuse dynamics. As well, interviewers rely on mental health professionals to offer guidance throughout the investigative process. The child's well-being and protection are paramount and should always be safeguarded. Again, one should know which mental health professionals in the community are familiar with child sexual abuse concerns.

Integration, coordination, and accountability are essential components in the intervention in child sexual abuse cases. In order that the victim receive adequate services encompassing the wide range of professional involvement, communication and liaison become vital to the process. This can only be achieved by a commitment on the part of those concerned to recognize and establish coordinating efforts between the various parties. All professionals play a pivotal role in initiating and organizing committees aimed at integrating services to victims.

CHAPTER FOUR
Initial Therapeutic Intervention

THE THERAPEUTIC INTERVIEW

There are situations where a victim of child sexual abuse will be interviewed to establish a need for treatment. Outside of investigative authority, these interviews are usually performed by mental health therapists or experts in child development. In order to assess the psychological needs of the child, the interview focuses on behavioural and emotional adjustment related to the abuse. Such interviews do not always follow rigid guidelines necessary in assessing risk or potential risk for court purposes. As a result, some direct questioning may be part of the interview.

It is essential that the therapeutic interview not take precedence over the investigation process. Such interviews are useful under the following circumstances:

1. The situation surrounding the incident has already been investigated and court action has occurred or is not likely to occur
2. The alleged offender is deceased
3. It has been clearly established that the identity of the alleged offender is unknown.

Purpose

The purpose of the therapeutic interview involves assessment with the goal of establishing a treatment plan. A possible interview strategy might include questions related to the offence, an exploration of the child's feelings surrounding the situation, indicators related to the level of the child's feelings of responsibility, and overall social skills. Such an interview could also include questions related to trust, safety, control, and support systems. In order to initiate an appropriate treatment plan, the therapeutic interviewer may have to inquire about different issues than in a criminal investigation. The interviewer is less interested in factual details and concentrates his or her efforts on the emotional impact.

Child Before the Court

Situations in which the child has completed the investigation process and is awaiting trial pose special problems for mental health professionals. While it may be weeks or months before a child may have to testify, treatment needs have to be addressed immediately. Consequently, conducting the therapeutic interview has the potential to contaminate evidence related to the trial. It is important that interviewers discuss this dilemma with Crown counsel prior to beginning treatment. This is not to suggest that the treatment needs of the child be delayed, but there are safeguards to ensure that the process will not interfere with the Crown's objectives. These safeguards could include non-leading questions and accurate record keeping with clear objectives defined. Individuals conducting therapeutic interviews may be required to testify about their treatment approach, goals and objectives.

Treatment Needs

In conducting the therapeutic interview, the special circumstances related to intervention may involve an evaluation which not only includes the situation surrounding the abuse but also how the child has experienced previous investigations. If the interview follows the trial, it may be very important to ask about the court experience. Many children require an opportunity to work through their feelings surrounding such a process. For some children testifying is therapeutic and for others it is traumatic.

Many children do not have the opportunity to appear in court. Should the alleged offender be deceased, questions surrounding the child's inability to seek resolution may be relevant. This is also a possibility if the identity of the offender is unknown.

Record Keeping

All interviews, whether therapeutic or investigative, should include some form of record keeping. Child professionals are advised to document the date, times, and places where the interaction with the child occurs. It is not uncommon for such cases to include unexpected information which could lead to an investigation, even if it did not seem likely at the time. This information may be extremely helpful in the event of a future trial because detailed recall can sometimes prove difficult. Outside of the criminal investigation, record keeping is beneficial in documenting an individual child's or family's progress. All information should be kept highly confidential and only shared with the individual's written permission.

CHAPTER FIVE

Counselling

TREATMENT DEFINED

Treatment varies a great deal, depending on a number of factors. These include effects of the abuse (see Chapter One), the age of the victim, the relationship to the offender, and the circumstances involved. Intervention can include individual counselling, family counselling, play therapy, group therapy, and others. Various therapeutic models have been well documented; however, there are few longitudinal studies reflecting treatment outcome.

Treatment usually begins at disclosure. Everyone becomes a part of the intervention system, and it is important to recognize that crisis intervention can provide the groundwork. Child professionals will need to help the child establish control and create an atmosphere of safety. It is important that during the crisis stage, individuals are aware of the need to establish trust. Children will need to know what is likely to happen in the immediate future. For young children, the events can seem scary and it is helpful to identify this for them. For adolescents, it is helpful to talk to them about the consequences of disclosure and for them to know that it is possible for the system to break down. Adolescents need to be aware that the following months may appear out of control, and again, it helps to identify this for them.

Child professionals need to understand that these children do not have the resources to change overnight. Offering information on self and others and creating a comfortable atmosphere are crucial in the intervention process. The problems to be discussed include the extent of the problem, medical and legal positions, and advocacy. Once the secret is out and the crisis hits, a child could appear relieved. As a result, the disclosure can often be misinterpreted as fabrication because the child is not exhibiting behaviour professionals believe to be indicative of victimization. Once relief wears off, it is not uncommon for children to experience tremendous guilt, fear, and anger. During this period, a child may exhibit school problems as well as behavioural disturbance. Again, it is important to assist children in identifying what is happening. Reassurance at each step in the treatment process is necessary.

Treatment considerations can include play therapy, relationship establishing, teaching touch limits, addressing learned helplessness, and issues related to self-esteem. There are standard treatment issues, and it is important to know when to use them. These include depression, suicide ideation, delinquent ideals, communication exercises, and value skills clarification. It is not uncommon for sexual abuse victims to be isolated from peers and their community. Therefore, these children need to learn to relate to other children. By teaching social skills and engaging the child in healthy, peer-related activities, the child will lean alternative forms of interaction. Common, and perhaps the most important, issues to address include age appropriate concerns related to sexuality, coping skills, and helping the child deal with fears, however irrational they may appear.

As a result of the sexual victimization, many children experience a high degree of powerlessness in their lives. It is extremely difficult to acknowledge that the breach of trust in any relationship has resulted in a sense of being used and exploited. Consequently, a major goal in treatment involves empowering children to feel more in control of their lives and to regain their sense of self-worth. For many victims of sexual abuse, all forms of expression, verbal and non-verbal, may be inhibited. The counsellor can assist in identifying and recognizing feelings which have been rejected in the past. This may be a result of the child's inability to trust and the degree of shame experienced. As children gain a greater awareness of the effects of abuse, they are able to redefine problem areas for themselves and create new alternatives.

Individual Therapy

Individual therapy and treatment strategies greatly depend on the child's developmental level and cognitive capacities. For young children, play therapy has been treatment of choice due to their inability to verbalize. Adolescents, on the other hand, have an increased ability for self-expression and can benefit from verbal interaction. It is important to remember that not all sexual abuse victims require treatment. Professionals providing treatment services base their decisions on a number of factors:

— child's ability to discuss the abuse
— level of responsibility and shame related to the abuse
— ability to trust
— present peer and adult relationships
— ability to assert individual needs
— level of support within the family
— degree of behavioural disturbance
— emotional indicators: depression, suicide ideation, self-injurious behaviour
— school performance
— social skills exhibited.

These factors are not necessarily indicative of sexual abuse, and child professionals must exercise caution in reaching this conclusion prematurely.

Following an appropriate assessment, it may become apparent that these indicators are in fact a result of the exploitation. Individuals providing treatment must clearly identify the presenting problems and establish both short- and long-term therapeutic goals. Initially, individual counselling will focus on establishing rapport and trust between the child and the therapist. Many victims have little reason to trust, and extreme caution is critical due to the sensitive nature of the relationship. Many of the initial statements made by therapists are similar to those statements made by offenders. Adults must be aware of their language (both verbal and non-verbal) and not hesitate to inform the individual child that they would never touch him or her in a sexual manner. This statement reassures the child and is a stepping stone to building rapport and creating a safe environment in which the child will feel able to discuss difficult topics.

Individual counselling assists children in establishing more control of their lives. Empowerment should be considered at all levels of interaction. During initial sessions, children should be given choices surrounding the treatment plan. Therapeutic goals should be discussed openly and be subject to change depending on the feedback. It may not necessarily be in children's best interests to be told of their new-found power when in fact it does not exist in their home environment. Some children will need help making distinctions between different environments, such as home, school, friend's home, and the therapist's office.

For some children, sharing their experiences with a supportive peer group can have a positive, therapeutic benefit. Therapeutic groups are most beneficial, particularly when preceded by individual therapy.

Group Counselling

Group counselling may be divided up into specific age groups: under nine, nine- to twelve-year-olds and adolescents. For the younger group, mixed gender can be helpful, but this is not recommended in groups involving adolescents. Groups should be time limited (eight to ten weeks) and should not exceed ten participants. Co-leaders are preferred and it can be helpful if they are both male and female. It is important to always be sensitive to gender-related issues as individual children may feel more comfortable with the same sex therapist. The converse is also true.

In a similar way to individual counselling, group work is goal oriented and often task specific. There are many different kinds of groups, each with a specific emphasis. Some are therapeutic, educational, supportive, or a combination. The group's purpose will help establish specific goals and the related activities.

Again like individual counselling, group participants can be empowered to participate in establishing the initial ground rules, goal setting, and the resulting activities. Individual children can be encouraged to discuss favourite activities and how they may relate to the group's purpose. Continual openness about the group and its purpose will help to establish a level of comfort necessary for an effective response. Specific goals will enable group leaders to maintain a focus and evaluate outcome.

Topics vary depending on the group's purpose but may include the following:

— *Emotions*
  — identification and expression of feelings

— *Communication*
  — expressive and receptive
  — right to say no
  — assertiveness training

— *Anger Management*
  — explore sources of anger
  — establish alternative forms of behaviour

— *Fault and Responsibility*
  — explore sources of guilt
  — clarify various levels of responsibility

— *Control*
  — powerlessness and personal safety
  — learned helplessness

— *Sex Education*
  — difference between sexual versus affectionate behaviour
  — values clarification

— *Conflict Resolution*
  — separation and divided loyalties
  — termination of the group.

Whether providing individual or group counselling, there are many situations which require family intervention in order to effect change.

Family Counselling

The disclosure of sexual abuse is traumatic for the entire family. This is especially true if the alleged offender is a member of the family. Like individual counselling, crisis intervention provides the groundwork. Initially, families require information because many members harbour myths surrounding sexual abuse and its impact. Non-offending caretakers often experience similar reactions to that of the victims. Disbelief, denial, anger, and fear are all common responses related to disclosure. Concrete information can help dispel unfounded assumptions.

For incestuous families, goals of therapy may include working out the division of power regarding parental authority. The non-offending parent will require tremendous support as he or she struggles with decision-making based on conflicting loyalties while at the same time coping with isolation, stigma, and possible economic hardship. Many incestuous families are dysfunctional and exhibit a variety of symptomatic behaviours. It is not uncommon for such families to be isolated from the community and maintain traditional patriarchal prerogatives. All families maintain alliances, and it is important that child professionals never assume that the relationship between the child and the alleged offender is a negative one.

When the abuse occurs outside the family, the reaction is contingent on a variety of circumstances. These include the relationship between the offender and the child, the degree of emotional distance between the child and parents, circumstances surrounding the abuse, and reaction to the disclosure. Children whose parents respond in a manner which is supportive and non-blaming may not require treatment. There are times when the sexual abuse of the child evokes personal issues for the parents related to their own childhood, and consequently, adverse reaction may have little to do with the initial disclosure. Again, parents need information about child sexual abuse as well as an opportunity to discuss their feelings and reactions.

Often ignored, siblings of sexual abuse victims must be included in the recovery process. Shielding brothers and sisters from what has occurred can sometimes do more harm than good. Increased secret keeping within the family can simply perpetuate further vulnerability. The victim should be consulted and ultimately decide whether to include siblings in family counselling. The siblings may be integrated into the group later in the process and that should always be an option worth considering.

CHAPTER SIX

Treatment Strategies

KEY ISSUES

All effects resulting from child sexual abuse must be regarded as both individual and unique. Child professionals must be cognizant of a stereotypical response and avoid labelling or categorization of personal trauma. In seeking answers to difficult questions, individuals may develop assumptions based on generalities rather than the concerns exhibited by the child. Therefore, treatment goals are generated from the experience expressed by the child and not necessarily from what is known about sexual abuse. However, there are some central themes needing to be addressed which appear to be prevalent in the majority of cases. Such themes reflect the nature of the relationship between the child and the offender and the internalization of the experience resulting in shame and self-blame. Treatment strategies will be provided for some of these key issues which include the following:

— Consequences of disclosure
— Responsibility and self-blame
— Inability to trust
— Anger management
— Sex education.

Consequences of Disclosure

Rarely are children prepared for the chaos and confusion resulting from disclosure. This is equally true for families. Often a child's fear of disbelief and blame becomes reality and adverse reactions from those closest to the child compound the confusion. Due to high emotions and the degree of professional involvement, there is always the possibility of mismanagement. Consequently, a child's understanding of help and support may be further undermined, even though actions are taken in his or her best interests. During times of crisis, it is difficult to empower the child when such practical issues as immediate safety are being considered. Therefore, the consequences of disclosure become a treatment concern needing to be addressed early in the process.

Child professionals can address these issues both directly and indirectly throughout treatment. Children will need the opportunity to talk about what events led up to disclosure and their perceptions of what took place during and as a result of telling. This should not necessarily be viewed as an initial treatment approach as children will only be prepared to discuss details of disclosure once they have established trust. They may benefit from having the opportunity to role play their disclosure portraying the various players. Safety can be created by encouraging story telling using third person narrative and having the child complete the sentence (i.e., "Once there was a little boy who was very upset with the way his mother reacted when he told his secret."). Art work and puppetry are also mediums which help children express themselves (a child could be asked to draw a picture of how adults looked when he or she disclosed and encouraged to express the feelings associated with this).

Responsibility and Self-Blame

A very common technique used by offenders to elicit child cooperation involves encouraging the child to seemingly participate and make choices regarding the relationship. Children are no match for adult manipulation and coercion. A pleasurable, physical sensation reinforces the belief that the child is responsible for the interaction. Fault and responsibility are the most difficult stigmas to overcome for a variety of complex reasons. Child professionals will need to understand these complexities in order to effectively intervene. There is literature to suggest that once a child discloses, professionals should respond by believing the child and telling the child, "It is not your fault." From a therapeutic perspective this should no longer apply. Children often feel responsible, and to suggest otherwise can simply invalidate their feelings and undermine trust.

Second, feeling responsible may in fact be a coping mechanism. Individuals will accept responsibility for the things that are done to them as a way of not feeling helpless. Removing this coping mechanism (i.e., feeling responsible) may be reinforcing helplessness, which in many cases is worse than feeling responsible. Helplessness implies worthlessness and the consequences of not validating legitimate feelings can seriously jeopardize the helping relationship. This is in no way to suggest that children are responsible for the sexual activities perpetrated by adults. Issues involving fault and responsibility should be approached with caution and viewed as a therapeutic process and not simply seen as a statement of fact.

Role play and story telling are effective treatment strategies to address issues related to self-blame. Such techniques are productive when used with everyday, non-sexualized examples. Whenever an adult engages a child in illegal behaviour, it leads to confusion and often frustration. In order to address issues of responsibility, it is helpful to be creative and consider the following role play:

> An adult is in a department store with a young child and sees a watch in a display case. The adult asks the child if the child likes him. When the child responds affirmatively, the adult says: "If you really like me, you'll steal the watch, but you don't have to if you don't like me that much. It's up to you." When the child appears bewildered, the adult continues by saying: "I'm not asking you to steal the watch if you don't like me that much. If you like me as much as I like you, you'd steal that watch for me, but I'm not asking you to steal."

This is the type of subtle coercion with which children cannot compete. When the child steals the watch, he or she can then be asked whose fault it was that the watch was stolen. Most children are able to recognize at the time that they were manipulated and can often make the connection between this example and their abuse.

Other treatment strategies could include games, such as "Whose Fault Is It?" This involves providing a series of situations similar to the above example which provide the adult with opportunities to discuss the principles related to personal judgments. Often, effective treatment does not supply the answers but does help the child arrive at his or her own conclusions based on alternative solutions.

Inability to Trust

The inability to trust is often the central issue for victims of sexual abuse. These children have great difficulty discriminating between trusting, caring relationships and those that are exploitive. An adult approaching the child in a friendly manner is suspected of having an ulterior motive. This is understandable given the nature of past abusive relationships. As children create their own coping mechanisms resulting from such experiences, they inevitably generalize their fears and distrust to those around them. These children need to learn to trust again. Such a process takes time, and caution must be exercised in order to assist in empowering their decision-making in establishing new relationships.

Building rapport, role modelling, and open, honest discussion are all tools useful in the therapeutic process. Victims are highly sensitized to adult actions, and consequently, they may react adversely to touch. Child professionals will need to possess a tremendous amount of self-awareness when touching children and be particularly attentive to whether or not they are receiving permission. While some experts argue that sexual abuse victims should never be touched, the fact remains that young children in particular seek out genuine affection. Such modelling can indeed be therapeutic, particularly for those children having difficulty distinguishing between affectionate and sexual behaviour. It is important to be mindful that many sexual abuse victims have learned to behave in a provocative manner and it is the adult's responsibility to model otherwise.

The process of establishing trust begins at the initial meeting. From a practical point of view, child professionals are well advised to always follow through in their commitments to the child, be consistent and fair in their decision-making and assist in problem solving. Establishing trust takes time and for some children it may not be possible to recreate the innocence of childhood. However, it is possible to create alternative forms of coping which will enhance a sense of self-worth.

Anger Management

Rarely are children given permission to express their anger. Consequently, such feelings are often repressed or are exhibited in behavioural acting out. Many victims of sexual abuse are very angry and such feelings are usually directed toward the following:

— anger at the perpetrator for what was done to them;
— anger at the reaction upon disclosure (from parents, professionals, friends);
— anger at themselves for allowing the abuse to happen.

These issues will need to be addressed throughout the treatment process, and it is helpful to assist children in identifying the source of their anger as well as providing safe outlets for expression. While children attempt to cope with their own feelings of anger (often confused with fear and guilt), they may need to understand that those who care about them also feel anger. It is important that children recognize that they may not be the source of others' anger.

Feelings of anger can sometimes be equated with loss of control. It is for this reason that children are hesitant to express the rage within. Therefore, child professionals will need to create an atmosphere of safety prior to approaching this topic. There are many useful techniques which can assist in the process. Children can be asked to identify various emotions seen on video or in magazines. They can be encouraged to discuss their findings in relationship to their own experiences. Role playing through the use of puppets or acting can also provide a safe mechanism for approaching the topic. Asking children to draw situations which make them angry will inevitably lead to pertinent discussion. These exercises must be goal directed and provide the child with alternative means of expressing anger in a safe and secure environment.

Sex Education

Sex education becomes an integral part of the treatment process in that sexual abuse victims can benefit from understanding what has happened to them. It is important that any information be age appropriate and in full cooperation with the child's parent or guardian. Prior to any discussion of sex education, the child professional must absolutely create a safe environment viewed from the child's perspective. As soon as sexual information is discussed, most victims will become uneasy and be reminded of the abuse. Therefore, it is always beneficial to state clearly to the child that what previously happened would not happen in this circumstance. It is often preferred to have a parent or co-therapist present. Child professionals can play a role in educating parents with the necessary information and developing a level of comfort so parents can effectively communicate with their children.

Sex education is more than lessons in reproduction. Sexual abuse victims have often been given false information related to their bodies as well as offender motivation. For many children it is difficult to see the differences between what is affectionate behaviour and what is sexual behaviour. Many offenders are also unaware. Child professionals need to recognize that children harbour many myths about their bodies and their sexuality. Consequently, prior to disclosure these myths arise out of isolation and the lack of a safe environment to discuss openly and honestly questions and concerns.

Depending on the child's age, circumstances of the abuse and gender, sexual role identification may prove to be an important area of discussion. This is particularly evident in male victims. If the offender is male and the child responded to the physical sensations, homosexual ideation will need to be addressed. If the offender is female and the child found the experience traumatic, this could also reinforce sexual confusion.

For some children, coping with abuse involves sexual acting out with adults, peers, and even younger children. This reinforces the importance of proper sex education in order to assist these children in recognizing and identifying their own behaviour and how it is affecting others.

However sex education is discussed, it must be done in a context developmentally appropriate to the child's age and capacity to understand. Information should be objective and factual, and child professionals should refrain from instilling personal values. This is difficult and should not be attempted unless the child professional is extremely comfortable with the subject matter.

CHAPTER SEVEN

Special Circumstances

WHEN THE OFFENDER IS IN A POSITION OF TRUST

Outside the role of parent figure or guardian, an offender in a position of trust can include any individual having some responsibility for children under the authority of his or her position, whether through employment or voluntary service. Unfortunately, adults who are sexually attracted to children may seek out positions in the community which allow them both access and authority. Individuals in positions of trust may include day care workers, sports coaches, babysitters, child and youth care workers, teachers, clergy, social workers, and any other individuals involved in working with youth.

Children are particularly vulnerable to the advances of such individuals due to the nature of their relationship and the high degree of trust between the individual and the child's parents. Cases involving individuals in positions of trust are not too dissimilar from incest cases in that victims are confronted with having to cope with issues related to divided loyalties. There is usually more than a single victim involved, and consequently, children who have not disclosed are often confronted by investigators because of information supplied by other victims. Due to the level of dependency created, victims may exhibit some protectiveness toward the offender and have great difficulty in participating in the investigation.

When a child has been molested by an individual in a position of trust, the child's entire family can feel victimized. Parents often blame themselves for having allowed the contact or innocently offering instructions to their child to comply with what was asked of them. Many adults feel betrayed and need help in sorting out their feelings of helplessness, anger, and guilt. Co-workers and colleagues of the offender experience similar reactions to that of the parents. Many adults struggle with the loyalties they feel toward a friend, while at the same time feeling a need to protect the children involved.

A further trauma related to sexual abuse by a person in a position of trust has to do with the position itself. Many times children are unable to discriminate between the individual and the individual's profession. Abuse by a member of the clergy can be generalized to have a negative impact on all clergy, the church, or even personal, spiritual growth. Likewise, children who value education or sports could have their aspirations shattered by similar generalizations based on the betrayal of trust.

All of these concerns will have to be addressed during treatment, and child victims will need ample opportunity to explore this area.

When individuals in a position of trust are charged with an offence, it is not uncommon for the media to report various details to the public. Although a ban on publication can protect names, having a situation placed in the public eye can often be very traumatic and must be handled delicately. Additional support is required throughout a trial. Some benefits of media coverage include other children coming forward and disclosing abuse by the same or a different perpetrator. Without the publicity, these children may not have felt they had the permission or opportunity.

MULTIPLE VICTIM CASES

When large numbers of children have been victimized by a single offender, there are special implications which need to be considered by all professionals whether involved in investigation or treatment. These cases can prove to be highly complex and, due to the nature of disclosures, have a tendency to escalate. Often investigators are not certain of the magnitude of the problem until inter-agency coordination has been established. Nowhere is teamwork and communication more essential than in multiple victim cases.

The first priority should be to establish what resources exist within the community where the abuse has occurred: child protection, law enforcement, Crown counsel, medical personnel, and mental health professionals. Conducting the investigation and assessing the treatment needs of children and their families can be done cooperatively and coordinated within the team. It is important to address therapeutic needs while at the same time being cognizant of the efforts of law enforcement and Crown counsel. In communities where some resources are lacking, it may be necessary to utilize the expertise of professionals from other regions. This should be done with the needs of the whole community in mind, especially when dealing in a rural area. Any intervention must be coordinated and consistent, and confidentiality is vital.

Responding to multiple victim cases requires a wide range of intervention techniques. This could include the following:

— establishment of inter-agency team
— initial interviewing
— establishing treatment plans
— individual counselling
— parents' support group
— children's support group
— public information meetings

— local staff training
— media control.

Establishment of an inter-agency team is most important for monitoring the ongoing investigation as well as treatment progress. Someone should be appointed as coordinator, overseeing the various agreed-upon tasks and disseminating information. Although many disclosures may have occurred since the establishment of the team, formal interviews should be conducted only by those with investigative authority. Use of video camera and audio tapes may be recommended. Recent changes in Canadian law may allow such evidence into the court. It is useful to establish treatment plans in conjunction with investigators in order to maintain a consistent approach. This can include individual child counselling, group work, parent counselling, and family therapy. It is not uncommon in smaller communities for misinformation to be circulated. Public information meetings are a useful mechanism for establishing trust within the community and also for providing information in order to dispel unnecessary rumours. In communities with few resources, it is always beneficial to assist in establishing and increasing local expertise. Professional in-service can be provided to local professionals (teachers, nurses, doctors, etc.), allowing for future community self-reliance. Within an inter-agency team, it is always useful to appoint a single individual to respond to the media. This should be an individual with investigative authority, such as a police officer.

CULTURAL CONSIDERATIONS

There is little researched and written on child sexual abuse and its impact on differing cultural norms and values. When working with victims within a multicultural society, cultural awareness is important, particularly when discussing personal topics such as sexuality. Child professionals will need to acknowledge that there are many dissimilar norms within and among all cultures related to sexuality and how it is expressed. Increased awareness of the unique cultural values and sensitivity to different expectations can also assist in providing much needed advocacy. Depending on an individual's background, it is probable that the state is not seen as having a role in family issues. There is a problem understanding that children have rights and that professionals could intervene on their behalf. Consequently, all levels of intervention will need to be understood from the client's perspective.

Families of minority background may require special assistance in their attempts to understand the many systems involved in child sexual abuse cases. In providing such assistance, professionals will require an awareness of cultural boundaries, a greater degree of listening skills, and the ability to interpret and respond to non-verbal language. It is vital that those involved with intervention possess a thorough knowledge of how power is used in relationships. Many times, minority groups have had reason to lack trust in professionals; fear and confusion exist at some level even without a crisis. Allegations of sexual abuse compound these problems and must be handled very delicately. The various systems aimed at intervention (child protection, justice) can be very intimidating even when the language is understood. Language barriers may require the use of an interpreter.

It is important that the use of an interpreter be carefully considered. The following guidelines may be useful:

1. An interpreter should have some knowledge of sexual abuse dynamics and respond appropriately and sensitively, particularly during disclosure.
2. Interpreters should not be family members; emotional objectivity will need to be maintained. Due to the sensitive nature of sexual abuse cases it is preferred that an interpreter also be an experienced counsellor.
3. Professionals should continue to assess the client's level of comfort with the interpreter.
4. Confidentiality should be discussed at the onset in the presence of all parties.
5. Feedback should be encouraged by continually summarizing what has been understood.

Other areas to be particularly sensitive to are the all-too-common preconceived notions leading to stereotyping. It is important for professionals to examine their own belief systems and explore the origins of such beliefs, which often lead to value judgments. Confusion exists resulting from cultural issues and social class concerns. Many families of minority background suffer from poverty, creating additional sets of problems. On many occasions, cases of child abuse are results of the stresses brought on by poverty yet are often viewed as cultural.

Parental history, family function, and gender rights vary considerably from one culture to another. Child professionals will benefit from gaining insight into these differences prior to intervention.

FALSE ALLEGATIONS

Most professionals who work with children are concerned about false allegations. While most experts in the area of child abuse believe children, many view the idea of false allegations as a backlash against the rights of children. This issue is so controversial that many assumptions are made, creating further confusion and more questions than answers. It is extremely difficult to assess how often a false allegation occurs. A criminal acquittal is no measure of innocence because the rules of evidence are quite specific. Retraction is also a poor indicator because this is a likely occurrence once a child recognizes the repercussions of disclosure. Although there is some indication that there have been isolated incidents encouraged by other adults in child custody cases, again this is extremely difficult to assess. There are experts researching the whole area of children's credibility and how to validate their statements. It is likely that this will be a topic of controversy for some time to come.

The seriousness of any sexual abuse allegation requires highly trained experts to assess and make the vital decisions related to apprehension and recommending laying charges. Once an allegation is made, all interviews should be completed by a trained expert with the authority to act on a disclosure. The investigator will assess the environment and conditions under which the disclosure was made. The child's history and circumstances surrounding the disclosure will be taken into consideration. Specific details, the emotional condition of the child, the relationship to the offender, and behavioural changes are some of the considerations a trained investigator will examine. However, there are situations where it is the child's word against the alleged offender's. In all cases where the accused is a professional, in a position of trust, a protocol should be in place in order to respond effectively. In any institutional setting (schools, day care settings, residential care), there will be many individuals with the authority to investigate suspected cases of child sexual abuse. These may include a supervisor, child protection, police, community care licensing, school superintendent, or even parents. These individuals need to be coordinated, and more importantly, someone needs to be placed in charge. It is recommended that the protocol be established as part of agency policy and not as a response to a crisis. The following suggests a sample protocol designed to expedite an investigation in order to uphold the rights of the child and the accused.

Model Protocol
Responding to Sexual Abuse Allegations

1. The allegation is made.
2. Allegation reported to child protection and police.
3. Parents informed of the allegation.
4. Administration informed of the allegation.
5. The accused suspended with pay.
6. Meeting of investigative bodies: administration, community care licensing, police, child protection.
7. Team coordinator appointed. Duties: clarifies roles, sets deadlines, communicates relevant information to all parties, arranges meetings, and oversees that accurate records are kept.
8. Completion of investigation: Employee informed of outcome, reinstated or charges recommended, parents informed of outcome.

Appendix I

Canadian *Criminal Code* Sexual Offences

s.151   Sexual interference

s.152   Invitation to sexual touching

s.153   Sexual exploitation

s.155   Incest

s.159   Anal intercourse

s.160(1) Bestiality

s.160(3) Bestiality with children

s.163   Corrupting morals

s.170   Parent or guardian procuring sexual activity

s.171   Householder permitting sexual activity

s.172   Corrupting children

s.173(1) Indecent act

s.173(2) Exposure to children

s.212(2) Living off juvenile prostitute's income

s.212(4) Sexual services with juvenile prostitute

s.271   Sexual assault

s.272   Sexual assault with a weapon, threats to a third party or causing bodily harm

s.273   Aggravated sexual assault

Further Reading

Bass, E., & Davis, L. (1988). *The Courage to Heal: A Guide for Women Survivors of Child Sexual Abuse.* New York, NY: Harper & Row.

Butler, S. (1978). *Conspiracy of Silence.* San Francisco, CA: Volcano Press.

Coulborn Faller, K. (1988). *Child Sexual Abuse: An Interdisciplinary Manual for Diagnosis, Case Management, and Treatment.* New York, NY: Columbia University Press.

Finkelhor, D. (1986). *A Sourcebook on Child Sexual Abuse.* Beverly Hills, CA: Sage Publications, Inc.

Gil, E., Ph.D. (1980). *Outgrowing the Pain.* Walnut Creek, CA: Launch Press.

Groth, A.N. (1979). *Men Who Rape: The Psychology of the Offender.* New York, NY: Plenum Press.

Herman, J.L. (1981). *Father-Daughter Incest.* Cambridge, MA: Harvard University Press.

James, B., & Nasjleti, M. (1983). *Treating Sexually Abused Children and their Families.* Palo Alto, CA: Consulting Psychologists Press, Inc.

Jewett, C.L. (1982). *Helping Children Cope with Separation and Loss.* Boston, MA: The Harvard Common Press.

Lew, M. (1988). *Victims No Longer: Men Recovering From Incest and Other Sexual Child Abuse.* New York, NY: Nevraumont Publishing Co.

MacFarlane, K., & Waterman, J. (1986). *Sexual Abuse of Young Children: Evaluation and Treatment.* New York, NY: The Guilford Press.

Porter, E., M.A. (1986). *Treating the Young Male Victim of Sexual Assault: Issues and Intervention Strategies.* Syracuse, NY: Safer Society Press.

Waxler-Morrison, N., & Anderson, J. (Eds.) (1990). *Cross Cultural Caring: A Handbook for Health Professionals in Western Canada.* Vancouver, BC: The University of British Columbia Press.

Wyatt, G.E., & Powell, G.J. (Eds.) (1988). *Lasting Effects of Child Sexual Abuse.* Newbury Park, CA: Sage Publications, Inc.

Index